Praise for
Does God

"Whether you're ⣿⣿⣿⣿⣿⣿ seeking your next ⣿⣿⣿⣿⣿⣿⣿⣿ ...ship, or a professional athlete, you're sure to discover a new level of freedom in competition. Get ready to enjoy the journey as Bob Schindler leads you to think through what the Bible says about this subject, rather than merely giving you an answer."

Evan Albertyn, *Associate Pastor, Central Church of God and former South African national champion bi-athlete*

"Bob nails some of the internal gyrations many of us experience in sports and in life, and then surprises us with his answer. God cares deeply, but in ways more profound and life-changing that I had considered. This book might change how you think about your golf game or your next promotion."

Palmer Trice, *Founder and Director, The Barnabas Center*

Praise for
Does God Care Who Wins?

"Finally, a book that helps coaches, athletes, player and fans understand God's care for us and his goal to redeem us back to himself through sports."

M.L. Woodruff, *Sports Outreach Minister at Istrouma Baptist Church, Baton Rouge, Louisiana*

"I believe that one of the greatest historical heresies of the church is the idea that God cares about some things more than others... Schindler raises the important question of what really matters to God. His answer just might change the way you see every aspect of your life."

Dave Huber, *Director of Leadership Development, Made to Flourish*

"*Does God Care Who Wins?* has changed the way I play, coach, and watch sports. As a result, I have a richer view of who God is and a deeper joy in my pursuit of sports."

Tim Briggs, *Community Groups Pastor, Church at Charlotte*

Does God Care Who Wins?

Bob Schindler

Copyright ©2017 by Bob Schindler

All rights reserved. Published by Bob Schindler,
Charlotte, North Carolina.

No part of this publication may be reproduced, stored in
a retrieval system, or transmitted in any form or by any
means, electronic, mechanical, photocopying, recording, or
otherwise, without written permission of the author. For
information regarding permission contact the author at
bob@doesgodcarewhowins.com

ISBN: 978-0-9991265-0-9

Book design by Carrie Givens, carolynclaregivens.com

Cover design by Rob Shoemaker, robshoemaker.com

Unless otherwise noted, scripture taken from the HOLY
BIBLE, NEW INTERNATIONAL VERSION®. Copyright
© 1973, 1978, 1984 by International Bible Society. Used
by permission of Zondervan Publishing House. All rights
reserved.

Passages marked NASB are taken from the NEW AMERI-
CAN STANDARD BIBLE®, Copyright © 1960,1962,1963,
1968,1971,1972,1973,1975,1977,1995 by The Lockman
Foundation. Used by permission.

Passages marked NIV 2011 are taken from Holy Bible, New
International Version®, NIV® Copyright ©1973, 1978,
1984, 2011 by Biblica, Inc.® Used by permission. All rights
reserved worldwide.

Table of Contents

Introduction

I had just played the best round of golf in my life.

The round came on the last day of the crucible of PGA Tour Qualifying School, or Q School as it is often called. According to John Feinstein, "The chances of getting from first stage to second stage to the finals and the PGA Tour are pretty close to 100-to-1....In fact, most of the players who enter Q School will never make it to the tour. Only about one-third of them will ever make it to the finals, and about half will never make it out of the first stage."[1]

I spent two years preparing for this, my first Q School. The top 15 would advance to the finals for the privilege of playing on the PGA Tour. After three days of play, I started the final day in 33rd place out of the 144 golfers. Teeing off, I felt the pressure and knew it would take something special for me to advance.

The events of that round were almost magical, but I didn't begin to realize that until I got to the fifth hole, the toughest hole on the course. After a great drive, I hit a one iron from 220 yards to 15 feet and drained the putt to go to 2 under par. "Game on," I thought. I went on to hit every fairway and 17 of 18 greens shooting what would become the low round of the day. Now I had to wait while the 32 golfers with lower scores who teed off after me finished their rounds.

I had a mixture of emotions in those 90 minutes. On one hand, I felt great excitement for the performance I managed in light of the challenge before me as I teed off that morning. I played other sports. I had been in other tense situations that included some anxiety but nothing like the nerves I faced at Q School. It was exciting to play well amid such pressure.

As each player finished and their total was posted, my position kept rising—31, 30...25, 24... 20, 19—and I was afraid. Afraid to hope. Afraid that if I hoped too deeply and wanted it too much, it would be yanked away from me. In the fear, I resisted the encouragement from fellow players about my round and their hopes it would be low enough to qualify. As my position continued to rise, I worked harder to downplay it all and keep at bay the hope that was trying to rise in my heart.

That wasn't all. My fear and self-protection went so far in those 90 minutes that I didn't practice putt, or hit any balls in possible preparation for a potential playoff. I didn't even touch my golf clubs, thinking that if I did so, my hope—no matter how small—would "jinx" my chances and bring on what I feared.

As the final group finished and the results were posted on the scoreboard, I stood there in amazement. My round moved me from 33rd to a tie for 14th with five other players, dictating a playoff among the five of us for the final two spots, 14th and 15th.

It started to drizzle as the five of us headed to the first tee. The rain increased as we stood getting ready to tee off, so much so that I almost asked the official to delay the start. I didn't, nor did any of the other players, probably because we were all trying to keep a grip on our steadily growing nerves. Rather than focusing on the golf ahead of me, I was just trying to calm my heart rate and breathe so I didn't faint!

The playoff began. I bogeyed the first hole and was out. Just like that. After two years of preparation, four days of golf, four hours to play the final round, two hours of waiting—it was over.

The other four players headed to the next tee. I went in a much different direction as I trekked back to the clubhouse alone, what little hope I had now vanished. I tried to console myself and overcome my disappointment by thinking about the excitement of the good play that day that got me there. It wasn't helping.

Needing Perspective

I called my wife, Beth. While not at the qualifying site physically, she had been on the journey every step of the way. She heard about the first round bad weather and my good round that put me in good shape at 11th place after the first day. She empathized with my struggles during the second round when I got so physically sick that I considered withdrawing. She offered support as I bemoaned the unlikely chance of advancing because of the back nine that day which landed me in 65th place after day two. She encouraged me after better play in the third round that moved me up to 33rd after day three.

As I called her, I was aware of the 292 shots I had taken during the qualifying. I was aware of the reality that if my play had changed any one of those 292 shots up or down one shot, I wouldn't have been in the playoff. I would have either qualified in the 14th spot with those other 4 playing off for the 15th spot or I would be out of the playoff. If I hadn't gotten sick on day two, I would have advanced. Easily.

I was even more aware of the numerous ways in that last round that my score could have been lower. I left an uphill 8-foot putt for birdie on the 8th hole dead in short just on the lip. More frustrating, I left a 12-foot downhill putt for birdie on the 11th hole hanging on the lip in what seemed like an impossible resistance to gravity. I had a 10-foot birdie putt on 13 lip out and come back toward me and a 90-degree lip out on a 5-foot birdie putt on 15. If one of those putts had gone in, I would have advanced.

As I called Beth to tell her about what happened, in my mind was a very personal question—

"Did God care about the results that day?"

To put it another way, as the title of this book asks, "Does God care who wins?"

While this question may not be an important one for everyone who plays, coaches, or spectates sports, it was critical for me that day. This was not a theoretical question to be bantered about in bars, on sports TV programs, or in the media in general; this question was a very personal one.

Our Journey

At the time of Q School, my wife and I were young but growing Christians. A few years before, during our senior year of college, we were exposed to the life-changing truths of the gospel of Jesus Christ. We heard and understood for the first time that there is a Creator. We heard that this God who created all we saw deeply desired an intimate, personal relationship with us. However, we learned that a barrier existed between us and God that we could do nothing to overcome, no matter how hard we tried. The good news we found out was that while we couldn't do anything, God was willing to do anything to remove that barrier. Out of his love, he was willing even to send his Son, Jesus Christ, to live, die, and rise again to overcome this barrier to our relationship.

Those truths moved us. Deeply. In response, we accepted this offer from Jesus to do for us what we couldn't do for ourselves and became followers of Jesus Christ.

While the impact of our new relationship with God and his Son grew slowly at first, we learned more about Jesus and about what is involved in living as his followers. One of the important truths we learned through our involvement in a local church, small groups, a para-church ministry, and personal study was that Jesus Christ had a unique purpose for each of his followers in advancing his kingdom and values here on earth, not just for those in vocational ministry. As a result, after graduating from college and spending over two years as a chemical engineer in technical sales in the industrial chemicals business, we left business in pursuit of a career in professional golf in response to what we sensed was one aspect of his unique purpose for our lives.

We were now two years into the journey. Hopefully, you get a sense that as I called my wife that afternoon, this question, "Does God care who wins?" was a very important and foundational one for both of us.

Imagine you are my wife on the other end of the phone line that day and I ask this question, "Does God care who wins? Does he care about the results out there today?" You realize the seriousness of this question and the weight of your answers. What would you say? Would your answer honor the question and the heart behind it or would your response dismiss the question as silly or petty? Would it bring comfort to my disappointment or minimize my pain no matter how well intentioned? Would it honor God and draw my heart to him or leave me distant from him? Would it empower me to press in on the disappointment I felt that day or lead me away from further competition?

Many years later, I am a long way from the pursuit of professional golf as an expression of my unique purpose but not from the answer to this question. In fact, my passion today is far greater than it was back then. However, now my passion isn't just about my personal answer to the question. These days I am involved in sports ministry, particularly the expression of sports ministry in and through local churches in the United States and around the world. In that role, I get the opportunity to interact with thousands of players, coaches, and parents. I have found many of them for whom this question is also personal and foundational. This involvement has stirred my passion for others who wrestle with this question.

I write this book with them in mind and for all the others I haven't met who are more than casual in their approach to sports and spirituality. I write to you who are invested in both arenas and wonder at the integration of the two, who find the common answers to this question leaving you wanting.

Does God care who wins? It is a big question that needs unpacking. The issues and answers are more important than you think.

chapter one

Does He Care?

I get a little nervous speaking for God.

After all, he is infinite, all-knowing, and all-wise. I am finite, know very little, and am often quite foolish.

Yet, for three reasons, I feel compelled to speak to answer this question, "Does God care who wins?"

First, because so many others have spoken up on this topic, often with dissonant voices.

"Only God could do this!" Clemson University Coach Dabo Swinney declared in a post-game interview with an ESPN reporter after Clemson's historic win in the College Football Playoff National Championship game against Alabama in 2017.[2]

"I don't think so," said the Rev. George McGovern, an interdenominational minister who is team chaplain for the New York Giants and Yankees, when posed with the same question, "Does God care who wins?"[3]

To the contrary, Russell Wilson, the celebrated Seattle Seahawks quarterback, all but declared his team's stunning and historic 28-22 overtime victory over the Green Bay Packers in the 2015 NFC Championship Game a miracle.

"That's God setting it up, to make it so dramatic, so rewarding, so special."[4]

The following week, on his weekly radio show, Green Bay's Aaron Rodgers was asked a question about God's intervention in the outcome of football games, to which he replied: *"I don't think God cares a whole lot about the outcome."*[5]

Back and forth the declarations of God's involvement go. Not just among athletes.

"I don't see God's sovereignty operating in the outcome of athletic contests,"[6] says Rodney Reeves, dean at The Courts Redford College of Theology and Church Vocations at Southwest Baptist University, in Bolivar, Missouri.

To which comes the opposing retort, "God sovereignly uses athletic contests—and every other experience in life"[7] from Robert

Bergen, professor of Old Testament and Biblical Languages and chairman of the Christian Studies Division at Hannibal-LaGrange College in Hannibal, Missouri.

On and on it goes. "God cares!" from one camp. "God doesn't care!" from the other. In radio segments. On TV sports shows. In blogs. The debate continues. So much so that even one of the leading sports magazines, *Sports Illustrated*, picked up on it. In the February 4, 2013 Super Bowl issue, the cover had a picture of Baltimore Ravens linebacker, Ray Lewis, a self-declared Christian who voiced his opinion in the media of God's role in the Ravens roll to the Super Bowl that year. In the picture, Lewis is in a body of water up to his waste with his hands folded in apparent prayer. At the top of cover, the question is asked, "Does God care who wins the Super Bowl?" for an article by Mark Oppenheimer.[8]

Real Confusion

At the end of all this debate, we are left confused.

Kurt Warner, Super Bowl XXXIV's Most Valuable Player and proclaimed Christian, sums up that confusion, "Do I believe that as a son of God that my life is important to him?

No question about it.... But I don't know how exactly that fits into winning and losing per se."[9]

In my own addressing of this subject, I have asked hundreds, maybe thousands of players, coaches and parents this question. I have them indicate their answer by raising their hand. Right hand—yes. Left hand—no. While I have not precisely quantified this research, I am amazed how consistent the results turn out. 50% "no," 50% "yes." Time after time.[10]

Yet amidst these adamant answers, I find a lack of depth. One might say that the nature of the question itself calls for a simple yes or no answer, but when I ask people why they hold either position, what I often get are platitudes that show a lack of clear, rational, and deep thought in their answers.

This simplicity is demonstrated by Brigham Young University football wideout Austin Collie when he said, "When you're doing what's right on and off the field, I think the Lord steps in and plays a part. Magic happens."[11]

This, after BYU beat arch rival Utah for the 2007 Mountain West Conference title.

Could the formula actually be that simple?

Rather than offering more simple answers here, what I will try to do is examine the complexity of the question and the implications of answers given. I do this with the hope of stimulating honest and deep dialogue rather than bringing that dialogue to an end.

Significant Division

There is another result of this current debate. We are not only left confused; we are also left divided. In the simplicity, the dialogue has turned to dogma. As one sports columnist wrote, "I refuse to believe that God—*anyone's God*—has a rooting interest in the outcome of something as secular and perverse as a [football] game" (emphasis mine).[12]

The debate has become a diatribe from both sides. After receiving significant criticism for his comments (see above), Austin Collie responded, "For people to make an issue out of saying that the Lord helps me out is ludicrous."[13] From the other side— "Thanking God from the winner's circle has become so common that one British newspaper published a letter to the editor entitled: 'Leave me out of your petty games –Love, God.'"[14]

Do you sense the divide?

This brings me to my second reason for writing. I write with a desire to bring mutual respect to this honest and deep dialogue. No one has a "lock" on the truth. We are all, even the best of us, looking through a glass dimly.[15] We need to humbly acknowledge our limitations and listen to what others have to say and attempt to understand why they say it. I write to appeal for that humble movement toward others.

I have one more reason I write. I write to see people move toward God.

In the humble and respectful dialogue I seek, we are not left to our opinions alone on this question. I come from the perspective that the Creator of everything we see and know is a personal being. As a personal being, he communicates. He has done so through a variety of ways including the world around us, the Scriptures of the Old and New Testament and most fully in the Word of God become flesh, Jesus Christ. While very comprehensive, this revelation from God doesn't speak directly to all issues, all questions, including the question addressed here. It does, however, give truth that can be applied to all life, what we call *wisdom*.

This wisdom comes from a process of study, prayer, and interaction with others.

You may or may not share in this perspective. If not, I am committed to respect you and your perspective and hopefully convey that respect here. I desire to dialogue with you about your view of God, whatever that is.

Honestly, I have wrestled for some time about whether to write this book. In Psalm 96 in the Old Testament of the Bible, the author commands, "Declare his [the Lord's] glory among the nations, his marvelous deeds among all peoples."[16] The command and heart behind this passage brings clarity to my motivation and overcomes my reluctance to speak on God's behalf. The passage assures me that this glory, this magnificence, has been revealed and can be spoken about from an informed viewpoint.

I want to say up front: this book is really more about God than it is about sports. (For that matter, all of life is more about God than it is about whatever else we think it is about at any moment in time!) Don't get me wrong. The book is not just about God. It is about the integration of sports and God, but at the heart of the question is the nature of God and his view of sports. While I love the question of this book, what I really value is how this question exposes much of what we think he is like, his heart is like.

This view of God's heart is important. It impacts the way our heart responds to him. We are moved toward or away from him depending on how we see his heart.

A Common Struggle

I was sitting on a bus recently with a high school sports chaplain. He is in his late 30s and works for a well-known para-church ministry for students. As we got to know each other, I could see he takes his role very seriously. He understands his influence. He knows many of these athletes are at a critical time in their lives where long-term goals are formed and pursued with significant lifelong impact. He wants to help them, to serve them, to love them as he comes alongside them.

We talked further about what he does in his role. One aspect of that role is to pray with the teams. He admitted honestly, "When I pray with these teams before the games, I often wonder, 'Does God really care about all this?'"

Because he is confused about this question, he is stuck not knowing whether to move on to other prayer topics or pray more fervently about the game's outcome, pressing into God's heart.

After listening, I affirmed the challenge of the question. We talked about the impact of this confusion as seen in his life. I shared some of my own journey in answering the question. We discussed the possible answers. Finally, I shared my thoughts—thoughts I will outline in this book.

As I have found with others, these thoughts clarified much of his confusion and moved him toward God. It did so not because of some human wisdom but because it fulfilled what the Psalmist calls us to do—to declare God's glory. This glory has a beauty, a magnificence that is compelling to our hearts.

Our movement toward this compelling glory comes with great impact. Not only does it honor God, it satisfies our hearts. More important to our discussion, it reorients our sports from the typical man-centered approach to a God-centered one.

If that process sounds like an intriguing one, that's because it is! The process of moving toward and connecting with this magnificent God, along with helping others to do the same, has been the greatest adventure of my life. I write with the hope of seeing many others launched into similar pursuit.

Toward that end, let's take a look at the typical answers to the question and their troubling implications.

chapter two

No, He Doesn't

"Spiritually, God doesn't give a rip if I win or lose."

This declarative "NO" in answer to our question comes from Jay Wilson, former chaplain for the Pittsburgh Steelers.[17]

Others chime in adamantly.

"It is absolutely ludicrous to think that Almighty God has any interest in the score of a football game any more than He cares about who wins when I play cards with my 92-year-old mom or play basketball with my 11-year-old grandsons," says Michael Brown who holds a Ph.D. in Near Eastern Languages and Literatures from New York University and has served as a professor at a number of seminaries. [18]

John Walters of NBCSports.com even goes as far as to say, "There are few things regarding religion that approach consensus, but it's fair to say that most of us concur with FoxSports.com columnist Mark Kriegel, who recently wrote, 'I refuse to believe that God—anyone's God — has a rooting interest in the outcome of something as secular and perverse as a [football] game.'"[19]

The first reason typically given for this answer revolves around the insignificance of sports. In this view, the world faces greater concerns like the refugee crisis, world hunger, sex trafficking, and preservation of the planet. Compared to these global, even life-threatening issues, our games don't measure up in importance. In fact, they are often called "petty."

If we think this way, certainly God must as well. "When you think of all of the issues the world faces and the interests that God has, we don't believe God really cares who wins or loses games and athletic competitions," states a blog post from the Active Faith sports website.[20] Others even seem to go as far as to say, "God doesn't care who wins. I mean, after all, he is the ruler of the universe. He has more important things to care about."

Espousing this, we are left with a God who has two buckets. One bucket with the label "God cares" and the other with the label "God doesn't care." In this argument, he puts those significant issues, like the ones previously mentioned or others like them, in the "God cares" bucket and our sports in the "God doesn't care" bucket.

Two Buckets

We follow his lead. We end up with the same two buckets. Just like God, we fill them up with things we think he cares and doesn't care about.

There is a problem with this thinking. Who decides what goes in which bucket?

I stood before a group of about 100 Division I college football players and coaches. I asked them the question, "Does God care who wins this game you are going to play tomorrow?" I asked them to raise their hand to indicate their answer, right, yes, left, no. Most said no.

Following their answer, I explained that I didn't want to focus on the particular idea regarding the game but on the general idea of what matters to God. I explained the two-bucket idea and gave them a list of different life activities. I then asked them to tell me what from the list went into the "God cares" bucket and what went into the "God doesn't care bucket."

I started with the "God cares" bucket. From the list, they picked items like prayer, Bible study, church, serving others, loving people, giving money to the less fortunate, and other items that we might typically label as "sacred" things.

In the "God doesn't care" bucket, they put eating the dinner they just had, putting on their uniforms, football and practicing for the game (the coaches may have had a different opinion on this but didn't speak up), the outcome of the game, attending and studying for classes (if their parents were there, they would have definitely voted differently on this one!), and other activities we might typically label as "secular."

There was general agreement to these answers. Not much pushback.

To the question, "Who decides what goes in which bucket?" the answer is, "We do." Whether we have identified it or not, my experience is we each have a pecking order, a priority, of what matters to God and what doesn't. We all have items in each of the two buckets.

GOD CARES
SACRED

GOD DOESN'T CARE
SECULAR

This perspective—known as the secular/ sacred dichotomy—is not a new one. It is centuries old and has been held by proponents of many different philosophical and religious views including the Greeks and the Hebrews. In Christianity, we might even point to the monastics as those who live this view to an extreme, withdrawing from all they see as "secular" to devoting their lives to the "sacred."

Today, we label this dichotomy a compartmentalized view of life. We may not go to the radical extremes of others in the past, but just like them, we have our compartments. The coaches and the athletes I mentioned have them. Often, so do those who hold this view that God doesn't care who wins. Remember how John Walters even labeled our football as "secular and perverse."[21]

This view leaves us with a theoretical struggle about what goes in what bucket and we are left with a personal one. We wonder, "What does God care about in my life? Does he care about the things in my life that matter to me?"

What Matters?

Can you identify with this struggle? Think

about the Super Bowl for example. Think about how important the Super Bowl is to the fans of the teams who were playing. What about to the players, coaches, owners and their families whose career success is definitely on the line? If God doesn't care about the game for those people, what else doesn't he care about in their lives? Closer to home, what doesn't he care about in your life?

- Does he care about whether you get the job you are applying for?
- Does he care whether the sellers accept your offer to buy your dream house?
- Does he care about your schooling and the grades you achieve or the scholarship you are pursuing?
- Does he care about your children's grades, their scores on entrance exams and where they will go to college as a result?
- Does he care about the results of your mom's upcoming MRI?
- Does he care about the closing of this deal for your business?
- Does he care about this book I am writing about what he cares about?

In questions like these (or however you

would fill in the blank on "Does God care about my _____?"), I have found the same confusion as I have found in answer to the question, "Does God care who wins?" We just aren't certain what goes into which bucket. "After all, who knows what He cares about?"??

For the last 30 years, I have asked people in business, "What does God care about with regard to your job?" The top two answers I get are:

- "God cares about my job for the money I make from the job that can be given to fuel his purposes."
- "God cares about the relationships I build through my job, specifically with those who may not have a relationship with him, so I can tell them about that relationship."

In the bucket of "God cares" goes our money, or a portion of it, and the relationships we build with those who don't share our beliefs. Every once in a while I get this answer, "God cares about how I do my job," and they add "my job attitude" to the "God cares" bucket.

Here is something amazing. In 30 years, I

have never had one person say that God cares about the product of his or her work. No one has ever put the fruit of their labor in the "God cares" bucket. Ever! This is just another example of how wide and deep this sacred/secular dichotomy, this two-bucket thinking goes.

The results of this two-bucket thinking are nothing less than tragic. Since many of these things we put in the "God doesn't care" bucket are important to us, we end up thinking our hearts don't really align with God's heart. In that light, rather than move closer to him, we move our hearts away from him. All the transforming power of a relationship with God is confined to the "sacred" things of life. We are left to ourselves in those things in the "God doesn't care" bucket—especially our sports.

Impacting Sports

Evidence of the result of such a move in the sports world abounds. In a 2013 *Sports Illustrated* article titled "In the Fields of the Lord,"[23] researcher Sharon Stoll of the University of Idaho quotes a West Point football player she interviewed, a member of a Christian ministry group on campus.

When asked about the role of intimidation in sports, this young man said, "Ma'am, my job is to kick them in the head, knee them in the groin, stand over them and tell them never to get up." Stoll then asked how the linebacker would play against Jesus. "Ma'am, I'm as Christian as the next guy, but if I'm playing Jesus the Christ, I play the same way. I leave God on the bench."

Do you see this two bucket thinking at work? When this young man puts God "on the bench," the way he plays isn't important to God.

This dramatically impacts the way he and others play. Negatively. Stoll's research since 1987 shows that the longer a person plays organized sports the greater the degradation of their moral character.[24] John Wooden once said, "Sports don't build character, they reveal it."[25] A growing problem of corruption and violence is being revealed these days in the world of sports, all sports. This corruption can be tied to the prevalent "win-at-all cost" attitude that so often is built on this secular/ sacred dichotomy that answers "No!" to the question, "Does God care who wins?"

In defense, some of you, at this point, may be saying, "While God doesn't care who wins, God does care how we play." Many who see the growing corruption and want to do something about it espouse this idea. They answer, like Herb Lusk, former player, now pastor and Chaplain for the Philadelphia Eagles, "That's a very shallow way of looking at it, that God would care who wins," says Lusk. "It's not who wins. It's, do you serve God by displaying your talents to the best of your abilities?"[26]

This is a common answer among Christians. While they may be uncertain about God's concern for winning, they are more certain that how we play matters. With that in mind, much like those who say how they do their job matters, they put "how we play" or "the players" in the "God cares" bucket.

However, while this approach may help some with the corruption of sports problem or with affirming the love of God for people, this perspective doesn't solve the core dilemma. We are still left wondering what goes in the "God cares" bucket and specifically what to do with our passion for winning. In addition, this view leaves athletes with a diminished view of their sport performance. If God only cares about my attitude as I play, then my sports performance, along with my passion for winning, goes in the "God doesn't care" bucket.

Passion for Winning

Dealing with this passion for winning is very important to almost all athletes, even the casual ones. If we say, "God doesn't care who wins but he cares for the players," these athletes are left distanced from God and on their own to manage their passion for winning. The result: they either suppress it as something bad or just let it out unfettered as something that doesn't matter anyway.

Any who have tried the suppression method know that, while it may help temporarily, this doesn't work long term. This passion for winning needs an outlet. If not handled properly, it will come out, many times inappropriately. When that happens, we are left feeling guilty, ashamed of our expression, repenting for our bad desire and trying harder to suppress it.

But our desire to win doesn't die. Our efforts of suppression leave us with segregated, not integrated, lives. We end up with an outer and an inner life, where outwardly we act like we don't care who wins but inwardly we long for victory. This dichotomy fuels hypocrisy and the tragic secret lives that so often characterize our culture and our Christianity.

The power of God that is so needed to transform our hearts, our lives, and our sports is kept sequestered in the sacred "God cares" bucket, quarantined from our hearts' desire to win. We are left unchanged and our sports are left unchanged because our hearts are left unchanged.

For those who have tried the other "unfettered" approach, another problem is created. Without some transformation, the corruption of our desire to win deepens. We become more and more passionate for winning and for whatever it takes to win.

Our pursuit intensifies but we are left unsatisfied, especially when the win comes our way. In 2005 Tom Brady said, "Why do I have three Super Bowl rings and still think there's something greater out there for me? I mean, maybe a lot of people would say, 'Hey man, this is what is.' I reached my goal, my dream, my life. I think, 'God, it's got to be more than this."[27]

Unchanged or unsatisfied. There has to be a different way.

God's Care

The Scriptures reveal a different and more hopeful design. This design is built on the expansion and exaltation of God's realm of care rather than the lessening or diminishing of it. It is built on putting more, not fewer, things in the "God cares" bucket.

In a discussion with his disciples about this very subject about what God cares about, as his disciples wondered if they themselves made it into the "God cares" bucket, Jesus faced this idea head on. He demonstrated to them how much God cares about them by telling them that "even the very hairs of your head are all numbered."[28] Jesus took a seemingly impossible and unimportant task like counting the hairs on someone's head and used it to show them the extent of God's care for them. Even the number of hairs on their and your and my head go in the "God cares" bucket.

Some who propose the "no" answer may do so from a concern of taking this "God cares" idea to an extreme, using God as a personal genie for our wishes. However, in their efforts to combat this American tendency to trivialize God, they can actually be led to the opposite of what they hope to accomplish. In saying "no, there are more important things to God," one could easily come to the conclusion that God has a limited capacity for concern and he efficiently chooses what is important, leaving no concern left for things like sports.

But what if we take this idea Jesus put forth and expanded it even further? What if God's care extends not only to the very hairs on our head but to every aspect of our life, from what we see as the most significant to what we might think of as the least? What if everything in our life goes in the "God cares" bucket, even our silly games and our passion for winning them?

The valuing of everything in life is seen in the care of good parents for their children throughout the world. To a young mother, is there anything insignificant about her newborn? The number of breaths? Their breathing patterns? Their different cries? The amount of food they eat? Even what they deposit in their diapers? Everything is important. Why? Because that mother loves her baby! Our Heavenly Father has far greater love and concern than the best earthly parents. He cares about everything in the lives of his children.

To follow this idea, the question naturally comes up, "How can God care about everything for everyone?" It is a good question. Only a God with unlimited, infinite capacity for love and care could have such a broad and deep concern. This reality is what we find that the Scriptures declare. In Psalm 36:5, the psalmist David declares, "Your love, O Lord, reaches to the heavens, your faithfulness to skies," speaking about the unending nature of both. The prophet Jeremiah reiterates this idea when he proclaims, "The Lord's lovingkindnesses indeed never cease, For His compassions never fail. They are new every morning"[29] (NASB).

Unlimited capacity eliminates the problem of God not having any concern left for "petty" things like sports. Unlimited, infinite concern never runs out of things to care about. It spreads over all of life, including sports and who wins.

The Scriptures reveal that God is not only concerned about everything because of his infinite love, but his concern also stems from his authority, his dominion over everything. In Psalm 24:1, the psalmist says, "The earth is the Lord's and everything in it, the world and all who live in it." Everything means everything, including sports. The apostle Paul, speaking about the authority of the Son of God, says, "For by him all things were created...all things were created by him and for him. He is before all things, and in him all things hold together."[30] All things means all things, including sports. Paul goes on further to say, "He is the beginning and the first born among the dead, so that in everything he might have the supremacy."[31]

C.S. Lewis piggybacks on this idea, "There is no neutral ground in the universe; every square inch, every split second, is claimed by God and counter-claimed by Satan."[32] God owns, is over, and therefore, cares about everything.

Our Response

This perspective—that God cares about everything—is why in the New Testament you have verses like

- "Whatever you do, whether in word or deed, do it all in the name of the Lord Jesus" (Col. 3:17).
- "Whatever you do, work at it with all your heart, as working for the Lord, not for men" (Col. 3:23).
- "So whether you eat or drink or whatev-

er you do, do it all for the glory of God" (1 Cor. 10:31).

Notice the common words or phrases in these three passages: "whatever you do" and "all." Notice also the connection of "all" and "whatever" to the typical "sacred" labels of doing something "in the name of the Lord Jesus," "working for the Lord," and "for the glory of God." The New Testament writers listened to Jesus. They got this idea that God has unlimited, infinite care and ownership about and over everything in the earth. With that understanding, they put everything in the "God cares" bucket, destroying the secular/sacred dichotomy. Why, they even went as far as putting something as trivial as "whether you eat or drink" in the "God cares" bucket. With that perspective in mind, certainly sports and winning and losing should go there also.

In saying this, I don't mean that God has equal concern over everything. The Scriptures reveal by both repetition and declaration the things God cares about most significantly, which include the marginalized, the broken, and the humble. The outlining of those different concerns and where they fall in priority is for another time.

What I hope for in this discussion is the

recognition that saying "no" to our question tends to limit God's infinite concern. In limiting his character, we are often left with a smaller God who leaves us wanting. As a result, we move away from him and our "passionate-for-winning" hearts are left unchanged and unsatisfied.

What we want, what we need, is a magnificent and mighty God whose heart has no limits to its ability to care and whose power has no limits to transform. We need the one who says, "If anyone is thirsty, let him come to me and drink. Whoever believes in me, as the Scripture has said, streams of living water will flow from within him."[33]

Rather than being drawn to this great God, saying "no" can move us away from him.

This is the reason I don't like the "no" answer.

To say "yes" to this question with God's infinite care and unlimited authority in mind, holds him high, speaks of his glory, his magnificence, as the psalmist demands, and moves us toward him and his satisfying and transforming person and power.

But I have to tell you, there are also problems with the yes answer.

chapter three
Yes, He Does

"I think God was a Packer fan tonight."

This tongue-in-cheek comment came from Aaron Rodgers, quarterback of the Green Bay Packers, after they defeated the Seattle Seahawks less than a year after the Seahawks' dramatic playoff win over the Packers.[34] His comment was seen by many as a shot at Seattle Seahawks quarterback Russell Wilson who remarked after that previous playoff game, "That's God setting it up, to make it so dramatic, so rewarding, so special."[35]

Others in sports go even farther in supporting Wilson's affirmative answer. "Some of the things that happened out there today were supernatural. God gave us the victory. I am just happy to be part of his game-plan. Sometimes things happen in such a way that you don't have an answer for them. I personally felt God had a hand in this," from Jannie De Beer of South Africa about their 1999 Rugby World Cup quarter finals.[36]

Among athletes and coaches, this chorus seems to be growing. We often hear it in post-game interviews that begin with the athlete or coach thanking God or giving glory to God for the victory or the winning performance. We also "hear" it in more subtle ways when athletes point to the sky after a significant (and even what might be called routine plays these days) play or score, seeming to acknowledge God as the one who made that possible.

Unfortunately, the members of this chorus seem to come mainly from the winning camp rather than the losing one. While I know that there are athletes and coaches, like Russell Wilson, who acknowledged God's role even in the loss,[37] the tendency, at least in the media, is to hold up those who say these things after a win.

This tendency can lead hearers to think that God cares more about the winners than the losers, favors the winners over the losers, even if those proponents themselves don't think so. After hearing this chorus, we can easily conclude that God rewards the winners with good play and circumstances that lead to victory and punishes the losers with poor play and circumstances that lead to a loss.

The fact that God is seen this way is troubling. The reason given for God's acting this way—of rewarding and punishing—is even more so. "Winning is the ultimate worldly good in the sports culture; therefore, since God does 'good' toward those who do 'good,' the team reflecting the most 'goodness' should win—or so the thinking generally goes," according to Ed Uszinski.[38] God is seen as someone who rewards those who deserve such rewarding for their hard work and "good" behavior. This God also punishes the lazy and the scoundrels.

While many hold to this idea without knowing or actually declaring it, some have even gone as far as to say things like we already noted Brigham Young University wideout Austin Collie said after BYU defeated their arch rival Utah 17-10 on a 4th and 18 play: "When you're doing what's right on and off the field, I think the Lord steps in and plays a part. Magic happens."[39]

"Though most people might cringe at the unsophisticated nature of this argument," according to Uszynski, "a recent Pew Religion

Research Institute article reports that 48% of Americans believe athletes of faith are rewarded with good health and success, and the number jumps above 60% for professing Protestant Americans, regardless of racial background. We assume that God will bless the righteous with scoreboard victories and leave the less righteous sorting through their own limitations—both physically and spiritually."[40]

The Heart of Christianity

This "God rewards the good people with wins and punishes the bad people with losses" perspective is at best a naïve misunderstanding and at worst a well-crafted distortion. Either way, it is not the heart of Christianity. Christianity, at the core, is a message of grace for the undeserving, the poor, the weak, and the needy. To reiterate this point, Jesus began his well-known discourse, the Sermon on the Mount, with these words, "Blessed are the poor in spirit for theirs is the kingdom of God,"[41] reminding us that poverty, not abundance, is the key to experiencing the kingdom of God. The apostle Paul reiterates this idea when he says, "For you know the grace of our Lord Jesus Christ, that though he was rich, yet for your sakes he became poor, so that you through his poverty might become rich."[42] In Christianity it is the undeserving poor who receive the kingdom and the riches of Jesus Christ, the King.

To demonstrate this point even farther, the writer of the New Testament book Hebrews gives us a list of those kind of people. Well known leaders in the Old Testament like Abraham, Joseph, Moses are held up along with the general mention of those who "conquered kingdoms, administered justice...shut the mouths of lions, quenched the fury of the flames."[43] In our day, we would certainly call these people "winners." If the list ended there, we might be tempted to believe God favors winners.

However, the passage goes on to mention others who "were tortured and refused to be released...faced jeers and flogging, while still others were chained and put in prison. They were stoned; they were sawn in two; they were put to death by the sword...destitute, persecuted, and mistreated."[44] While we might think of them as losers, the author lists this second group together with those "winners." He includes both groups in this "Hall of Fame of Faith." Winners and losers qualify.

The author further clarifies what qualifies them for this Hall, "These were all commended for their faith."[45] It was their trust in God and not in themselves or their efforts that God rewarded with this commendation. They were those, "whose weakness was turned into strength; and who became powerful in battle."[46] They believed that God would fulfill what he had promised to them in their poverty and weakness, not in their hard work and disciplined effort.

As Tim Keller reminds us, "The gospel is this: We are more sinful and flawed in ourselves than we ever dared believe, yet at the very same time we are more loved and accepted in Jesus Christ than we ever dared hope."[47] The weak, the poor, the deeply flawed, the powerless who have faith—these are the particular people the God of Christianity moves toward, empowers, and who experience his kingdom.

This is the message of Christianity.

A Needed Comparison

Let's go back to this message that God favors the winners and punishes the losers. Do you see how this message stands in contrast to the God of Christianity?

- His is a message of grace, but we can end up with a message of deserved favor.
- His is a message for the weak and the poor, but we can end up with a message for the hard-working and the strong.
- His is a message of unconditional love of God, but we can end up with a God who only loves the "lovely."

With this perspective, the message of Christianity is distorted and the God of Christianity is trivialized.

- The Almighty Creator alone is sovereign over all, but he looks more like a genie in a bottle granting the wishes of the most deserving.
- He is a God who, as Philip Yancey states, "loves people because of who God is, not because of who we are,"[48] but his love becomes conditional on the merit of the receiver.
- He is a God who reminds us that his "ways are higher than our ways" and his "thoughts higher than our thoughts,"[49] but his values take on a worldly tint,

especially regarding winning and losing.

"Hovering over this discussion is a predominant but twisted American value long ago absorbed into our sports culture itself: *Winning is everything in life, and losing is for losers.*"[50]

Pride

The diminishing of God is not without effect. Make God smaller and what often comes with it in the athletic realm is the expansion of the sport. Instead of a game, competition becomes life and death. It is good vs. bad, the righteous vs. the wicked. Competition morphs from a game of striving together between two teams into a war between two opposing armies.

Coaches and players adopt this perspective to motivate players and teammates. To fuel the duel, Bible verses speaking of warfare are quoted out of context and put on t-shirts or tattooed at the expense of distorting God, his eternal and inerrant Scriptures, and the sports themselves.

But what about the players and the coaches, how does this "favoring of the winners" idea impact them?

Think first about the winners. They leave the game and, if not careful, think they deserved to win. After all, "We worked hard. We prayed. We pointed to the sky when we scored. We even thanked God for the victory during the interview." I am not calling into question the intent of those who have done these activities. What I am asking is, "What is really going on in their hearts? Who is getting the credit there?" My experience is that if a person thinks God favors winners, it is easy for that belief to turn into an attitude of pride, feeling superior to the losers.

As I have looked into my own heart, whether in my athletic competitions or even in writing this book, I see this pride running so deep. It's one of those things Tim Keller refers to as "far more sinful and flawed"[51] than I dared to believe or admit. Yet is it there. I have even found this thought lodged deep in my heart, "God is really fortunate to have someone like me on his team." Hard to admit, but true.

During my first trip to Africa several years ago, I was struck with this reality. As I traveled among four countries in 3 weeks, I couldn't help but imagine how many great athletes lived there. They had all the ability.

They had all the desire. They had all the work ethic. All they lacked was the opportunity to show off those talents. As I reflected on this, I realized what a gift from God opportunity is, a gift we take so for granted in the USA, thinking we even deserve it.

Apparently, those of us in America aren't the only ones with this problem. The apostle James warns all of his readers when he says, "Now listen, you who say, 'Today or tomorrow we will go to this or that city, spend a year there, carry on business and make money.' Why you do not even know what will happen tomorrow. What is your life? You are a mist that appears for a little while and then vanishes. Instead, you ought to say, 'If it is the Lord's will, we will live and do this or that.'"[52] Entitlement seems to be a widespread problem! Maybe if we said something like, "Today or tomorrow we will practice and play our scheduled games and win the conference," then the verses might hit closer to home.

The declaration of James is clear. Life, along with the ability and opportunity to succeed whether in business or sports, falls under God's will and grace. Whether these things happen or not is a gift from him—a gift, not a deserved result. There is no room for pride here, only gratitude and humility.

In our relationship with God, pride is a problem. The apostle Peter warns, "God is opposed to the proud but gives grace to the humble."[53] Do you see the reversal here? We think God is favoring those who do good, but, in fact, if that perspective has led to pride, Peter is saying is that it places God in opposition to that proud person. I don't know about you, but I think that is a game I can't win!

Shame

What about the losers? How are they impacted? As one writer so poignantly put it, "What is a losing team supposed to say when the winning team gives God the credit for a win? I mean, it's a conversation stopper, right? Do they say, 'Yeah. We should have known coming into this game that we were only measly, unrepentant Philistines and that the chosen Football Team of God was going to rain down fire and brimstone upon our pagan heads.'"[54] Since they have been punished, they are left humiliated, wondering what they did to deserve God's punishment, distanced rather than drawn to the God who longs to come alongside and comfort them in their defeat.

Handling winning and losing is especially difficult for athletes and coaches—even parents. We tend to put so much into our sports, so much so that our very identity is tied to ours or our players' or our children's athletic achievements. In the wake of our winning or losing, we easily slip into thinking we are winners, intensifying our pride, or losers, intensifying our shame.

When our identity is tied to our performance, we lack a stability to our lives that is so needed in the variable nature of that performance. We ride the roller coaster of highs and lows, depending on the outcome of the most recent game or performance, longing for something better, something more solid, more secure.

I wish I could say this perspective was limited to sports, but it's not. "If we tell viewers that God's closeness equals winning a sports game, how are sports fans supposed to interpret their own private losses? Do they conclude that God must not favor them or else their lives wouldn't be so full of defeat?"[55] Because of our sports-crazed, winning-athlete-and-coach-worship culture, we often answer, "Yes they do," and this perspective spreads. The sick, the bankrupt, the infertile,

in fact, all the strugglers in this life for whom
victory seldom comes, are left to think they
have done something wrong and deserve
their loser lot in life.

Let's go back to the heart of Christianity.
God's heart is for these who feel weak, lost—
those who think they are losers. He wants
to pour his grace into these lives. He wants
them to experience his unconditional love,
to be far more loved than they ever dreamed
as Keller says.[56] He wants their identity to be
rooted in their relationship with Him with
all of its aspects including being his children.
Yet, influenced by this "God favors winners"
mindset, they think they are disqualified for
such favor, keep their distance from God, and
never experience the solid identity he wants
to give them.

Proud or ashamed. Up and down. In far
more arenas than sports. If we answer "Yes,
God cares who wins," it can lead to arrogance
or humiliation or both. I am not saying that
it has to or always will. What I want you
to consider is the potential impact of this
answer left unexamined. We can assign the
unlimited concern and love of God to the
winners, excluding the losers in the process.
We can become arrogant or humiliated, living

unstable lives with our identity set on performance. We can trivialize God and distort the message of Christianity, feeding the sports-crazed culture rather than appropriately dampening it.

This is why I don't like the simple "yes" answer.

I have already stated I don't like the no answer either. Hopefully, you are asking, "Then what answer do you like?" That answer is for the next chapter.

chapter four
A Qualified Yes

It is all about the glory.

Let's be honest for a moment. We care about who wins. In fact, it might easily be said that we care too much.

The reason we care about who wins is mostly about the pursuit of glory, our glory.

In my own pursuit of glory, I have found that it has two facets. First, glory means magnificence, beauty, splendor, greatness. Second, glory means honor or fame. The second facet is the response to the first.[57] And fame is intoxicating!

We want both. We want to win for the establishment of our greatness. We also want to win for the recognition of that greatness. We like to win. It feels good. We also like what comes with winning—the honor, the accolades. It does something in us to be "glorified" and the desire for glory is at the heart of all sports, all levels, all ages.

> "If winning isn't everything, why do they keep score?"
>
> –Vince Lombardi, former Hall of Fame coach of the Green Bay Packers and winner of 3 NFL Championships and 2 Super Bowls[58]

> "The person that said winning isn't everything, never won anything."
>
> –Mia Hamm, former US women's national soccer star, two-time Olympic gold medalist, and FIFA Women's World Cup winner[59]

> "If money titles meant anything, I'd play more tournaments. The only thing that means a lot to me is winning. If I have more wins than anybody else and win more majors than anybody else in the same year, then it's been a good year."
>
> –Tiger Woods, PGA Professional and winner of 14 major championships (second all-time) along with 79 PGA Tour wins (second all-time) and the only person to be named *Sports Illustrated's* Sportsman of the Year more than once[60]

"I'm a mad dog whose only concern is winning."

–Charles Barkley, TV sports analyst and former NBA player, three time Olympic Gold medalist, named one of the 50 greatest players in NBA history[61]

However, admitting this reality leaves many of us in tension.

The Problem of Glory

Christians sing songs about glorifying God, to honor him. We remember creeds that declare "Man's chief end is to glorify God."[62] We read and hear the repeated phrase, "It's not about you,"[63] driving home the point that life is about God. This is where the struggle lies—our pursuit of our own glory and the call to give God the glory.

I was talking recently to Ryan Souders, NCAA Division III Calvin College soccer coach, about this book. He reminded me, "Bob, we don't ask the question, 'Does God care who wins?' because we are afraid of the answer." We went on to talk about what he meant and the idea that if God cares, we are afraid it will be for very different reasons than we care. "If that is the case, we are afraid he cares a lot and will probably ask us to give up our competition as something not good. That is what we are afraid of."

An intern with our sports ministry exemplified this Ryan's claim. She was a Division I soccer player and, in the course of her time with us, the discussion of whether God cares who wins came up. During that discussion, she admitted she didn't want to think about the question out of fear that it would diminish her passion to improve as a player and to win.

This struggle is real, particularly among thoughtful, spiritually minded athletes. We may try to eliminate the struggle by not asking the question, but as the coach and the player reminded me, ignorance is not bliss. The tension doesn't go away.

We may try to resolve the struggle by denying God cares. We gravitate to the "no" answer to our question. However, when our competition stays our competition, we are left unchanged and unsatisfied as I outlined in Chapter 2. The tension is still there.

Or we try to resolve the struggle by answering "yes" to the question. There, we try to do the things that would get God on our side, to favor our winning, to get him in on the pursuit of our glory. We are still left in charge, attempting to manipulate God by our hard work, prayer, or other righteous activities. I have outlined problems with this approach in Chapter 3. Again, we are left with the tension.

The Story of Glory

In bringing this up, I want us to recognize this struggle. I want us to see how this struggle is at the core of the question, at the core of all sports, really at the core of all life. I also want us to understand this glory struggle, because that understanding is critical to the right answer to our question and resolving this tension.

Initially, I want to affirm that, while the struggle between the pursuit of our glory and God's glory has been there for a long time, it hasn't always been that way. To get some perspective, let me ask you, "How do you view Christianity? If you were to outline the message of Christianity, what would you say? Do you see it as a set of propositional truths like 'God loves people,' or 'Jesus died for sinners'? Maybe a list of dos and don'ts?"

If that is how you view Christianity, you

are seriously limiting the good news or the gospel message of Christianity. According to Frederick Buechner, "There is no less danger and darkness in the Gospel than there is in the Brothers Grimm, but beyond and above all there is the joy of it, this tail of a light breaking into the world that not even the darkness can overcome. That is the Gospel, this meeting of darkness and light and the final victory of light. That is the fairy tale of the Gospel with, of course, one crucial difference from all other fairy tales, which is that the claim made for it is that it is true, that it not only happened once upon a time but has kept on happening ever since and is happening still.[64]

How one views this Story impacts their ability to answer the question. When we limit the good news, the Gospel of Christianity, to a set of dos and don'ts, we also limit our ability to effectively answer our question. We end up with simplistic answers like those I submitted that don't satisfy our souls or glorify God. However, when we see the Gospel as the Story of all stories, as the Story from which all stories gain their source, we gain important keys to resolving our question in a soul satisfying and God glorifying way.

The Gospel, this Story, has been referred to in different ways. Pastor Randy Pope refers to this story as The Story of Glory.[65] Others have referred to the Gospel as the Story of Redemption with four chapters—Creation, Fall, Redemption, Consummation.[66]

To gain those important keys, let's briefly review this Story.

Creation

"In the beginning,"[67] in the chapter titled Creation, God made all there is. From nothing. He didn't need to create because he was alone. He made all of Creation out of his self-giving nature. "Creation was a way for God to spend himself."[68]

All that he made was good. His authority and care spread over all of his good creation. It flourished as it was designed to flourish.

In his creating, God made people, a man and a woman. He gave them a unique role in the flourishing design for Creation. God declares this role prior to his creation of them, "Let us make man in our image, in our likeness....So God made man in his own image, in the image of God he created him; male and female he created them."[69] God intended them for glory—a greatness, a magnificence—as his image bearers, unique among all of his creation. When he then makes them in his image, he endows them with this glory, or as the Scriptures states he "crowned him with glory and honor."[70]

At this point in the Story, there is no glory struggle. No tension. God gives glory to the people and the people give glory to God as they live and live out this design. Since God endows them with this glory as his image bearers, the people are confident in what they have been given. From this confidence, their focus is on others, not on themselves.[71] They move toward each other to express, not establish, their glory, this greatness God had given them, and to benefit the other and bring honor to the God who endowed their glory. In doing so, they flourish as image bearers for God, with all of creation responding in honor of that greatness

The Fall

Here, the Story radically changes and not for the better. In Creation, God gave the man and the woman great freedom to express his image over creation with one exception. With only one restriction, amazingly and foolishly, they doubt his goodness and rebel. They think it would be better to have all the glory of being his image bearers without God as their authority, their source, their guide. In doing so, they move away from God as they disobey the good God who had given them so much.

Great was the impact of this move. All Creation was corrupted. I struggle even putting into words the greatness of that impact in a way that doesn't diminish the reality. We see this contamination all around us and within us. We live with the breadth and depth of the defilement every day. No one escapes the desecration now resident around and within us.

Nothing was left unharmed including all people, every person. We have all been marred, defiled, broadly and deeply. One aspect of that corruption is our loss of glory, "for all have sinned and fall short of the glory of God."[72]

In our rebellion and our corruption, we are now separated from God, without the relationship we once had with him. With no source of confidence in what we have been given, we feel inadequate and wonder if we have what it takes, inwardly knowing

the truth and fearing exposure. Having left
the source we need to guide our expression,
we feel lost, disconnected, unaccepted, and
alone. We try and fail and feel the shame
of failure—over and over. This move from
God has cost us much, including our glory.
Because of that reality, while we may not
acknowledge it, even to ourselves, we know
something is not right.

From this place, we are on a search for
glory,[73] a relentless search to establish the
glory we once had, which we were endowed
with by God. Image bearers we stayed, but
the image is now flawed, marred. Our focus is
turned inward toward ourselves, rather than
outward toward others, as it was in the First
Chapter when their relationship with God
gave them confidence in their glory.

Here the struggle for glory is now fully in
place. We foolishly think to glorify God will
cost us glory. We still doubt his goodness and
move to make ourselves great. There is probably not a realm in life where the establishment of this lost glory is more clearly seen
than in sports. All the levels, all the awards,
all the championships are, at the core, an
attempt to regain our lost glory, to prove to
ourselves and to others something about this

lost greatness and honor that was ours in the First Chapter.

There is a problem with these efforts, however. We long for the glory, the greatness and honor, that we were given by God in Creation. This is the "most creaturely of pleasures—nay, the specific pleasure of the inferior: the pleasure of a beast before men, a child before its father, a pupil before his teacher, a creature before its Creator,"[74] as C.S. Lewis reminds us. However, the earthly glory we move to establish, no matter how great, can never fill the longing for the heavenly glory in our hearts.

We have already mentioned Tom Brady's admission of this reality, for this glory that we so passionately pursue in sports is transitory in nature. It cannot satisfy our deeper longing. The line is long of those who are honest and acknowledge the lack of satisfaction in this earthly glory.

God said it would be this way when he spoke to the man and the woman after their rebellion. He said life without him would be a life of pain, with failure and futility as significant marks.[75] Life without him cannot by design ever satisfy. "God made us: invented us as a man invents an engine. A car is made to run on petrol, and it would not run properly on anything else. Now God designed the human machine to run on Himself. He Himself is the fuel our spirits were designed to burn, or the food our spirits were designed to feed on. There is no other....God cannot give us a happiness and peace apart from Himself, because it is not there."[76]

The Story at this point is a tragic one. Without God, the happiness, peace, and joy of living out our glory as image bearers is now gone. We are left searching for, longing for something we cannot find here. We would be left in the struggle of establishing our glory—our glory vs. God's glory—unsatisfied in our pursuits, without hope of ever finding resolution.

God had every right to let it end this way—tragically.

Redemption

However, God's heart moved him to make right the wrongs, to restore what had been lost. As Philip Yancey puts it, "In a nutshell, the Bible from Genesis 3 to Revelation 22 tells the story of a God reckless with desire to get his family back."[77]

In that desire, God moves toward us.

He chooses Abraham and his descendants to bring about that rescue and redemption plan.[78] He even promises to make one of Abraham's descendants the Hero of the Story who would bring the restored blessings of the First Chapter of the Redemption Story not just to the nation of Israel but to all the earth.

For the next several thousand years, God keeps moving toward us. He works out this redemption plan through the nation of Israel, the nations surrounding her, through particular leaders and people, all leading up to the arrival of the promised Hero of this Story.

Every great story has a hero. So does this one. Jesus Christ is the Greatest Hero of any Story, remembering again that this "fairy tale of the Gospel" is true. Never were the stakes higher. Never was the situation more hopeless. Never was the need for deliverer, a hero, more felt.

This is why he is the Great Hero. Never has one paid such a price, for this redemption would cost him his life. He "did not come to be served but to serve, and to give his life as a ransom for many."[79] But it cost him much more than just his life, "who, being in the very nature of God, did not regard equality with God something to be grasped, but made himself nothing, taking the very nature of a servant, being made in human likeness. And being found in appearance as a man, he humbled himself and become obedient to the point of death—even death on the cross!"[80]

Never has one saved so many, accomplished so much. He "came to seek and to save what was lost,"[81] in order to bring "many sons and daughters to glory" (NIV 2011).[82] The Story of Redemption brings many effects to those who embrace it. It is important in our discussion that we see that one of those effects involves restoring men and women to the glory God designed us to have from the beginning. Resolving our struggle is founded on this idea: Jesus Christ comes to restore our lost glory.

When we grasp and begin to live in the reality of this truth, some significant things begin to happen, inwardly and outwardly. As we grow in our confidence in this glory Christ restores, we find freedom from the pursuit of our own glory. We also find that we are no longer at war with God for glory. We are more and more able to rest in his desire for our glory.

As this happens, we are more and more free to bring glory to him. This glory goes much deeper than just pointing to the sky when something good happens. God begins a great work in the depths of our hearts. Change, real change, deep change begins to take place. Not all at once and never fully complete, but the change is there. Noticeable change. Maybe first to ourselves, maybe to others. Nonetheless, our broken hearts are being healed. Our heart's orientation is pointing more and more away from ourselves and outward—to God and others.

In this Redemption chapter of The Story, the struggle doesn't fully go away. We still battle as the healing of our hearts progresses, never fully complete until the final chapter of the Story.

Consummation

In this chapter, God's "reckless desire"[83] is fully realized. The Great Hero's mission is accomplished in making "everything new"[84] (notice, not all new things!).

Fullness of glory awaits us in the Consummation: "Christ in you, the hope of glory."[85] Our struggle for glory is gone there, for "He will wipe every tear from their eyes. There will be no more death or mourning or crying or pain, for the old order of things has passed away."[86]

Is that because we will no longer compete and play games? I think not, and others agree.[87] It is because in those games, our hearts are fully healed and our glory fully restored as God again fully endows us with our promised glory. Our pursuit for God's glory is completely in place. There, we care about winning and losing but only in the same way that God cares about it.

The Challenge

In the meantime, we are still in the struggle of Chapter 3. I don't use the word struggle lightly. It's God's glory vs. our glory. The battleground is our hearts. Any who have tried to live for the glory of God recognize how constant and challenging this can be. Living out these ideas involves a demanding process that will never be fully accomplished this side of the Consummation. It requires honesty and self-awareness that is hard to face as we so quickly retreat and pursue our own glory in our hearts even when we may outwardly point to the sky.

Yet, it is different. Since God is no longer our opponent but our teammate in the struggle, he accomplishes for us in that struggle what only he can accomplish:

- Showing us where our hearts are still broken and oriented toward ourselves and our glory, attempting again to establish our glory
- Giving us the courage to honestly acknowledge that wrong pursuit
- Loving us there and with his kindness moving us to turn away from this establishment to the expression of our greatness for His glory
- Giving us strength to press on and stand against further challenges to this expression
- Changing our hearts over time to a greater and greater orientation to his glory

As we struggle, He also calls us to consider these struggles and the suffering they produce as "not worth comparing with the glory that will be revealed in us."[88] As we embrace this struggle and press on for his glory, we are moving more and more back in step with his purpose from the beginning, the First Chapter. "God's first commitment is to His own glory, and...this is the basis for ours....'God's chief end is to glorify God and enjoy His glory forever.'"[89] God is concerned with his glory—both the enjoyment of the magnificence of his greatness and the recognition of this magnificence.

Wins & Losses

From this perspective on the Gospel, we ask again the question, "Does God care who wins?" The answer is this:

"Absolutely, he cares—but for very different reasons than we typically do."

He doesn't favor winners over losers. He favors how winning and losing contribute to His glory. And they do contribute differently.

Winning challenges us to recognize how we still think we deserve to win, how much "better" we think we are than others, how much our winning is because of our effort, even when we outwardly thank God. Losing challenges us to recognize how we still doubt God's goodness, how much we still wonder if we deserved to lose, how great the struggle is to trust God in our disappointment, even when outwardly we are also thanking God.

God cares because of his infinite concern for his glory and the way that every competition contributes to that glory, even for the seemingly insignificant person and detail. From this concern, "His sovereignty extends to the sub-atomic level, where every part of every atom arranges itself in relation to every other according to his plans and purposes—all of this in a world where humans make real choices that matter and have real consequences at every level of society."[90]

Winning and losing are also part of his redemptive plan. The Hero of the Story, Jesus Christ, is currently about making everything new.[91] The plan for making everything new could be referred to as his redemptive plan. As his redemptive plan rolls forward, the Hero's greatness is more and more magnified. The Son gains greater glory.

Wins and losses have a role in the development of his plan. While we may not understand it at the time, he is using them both to accomplish his purposes. "Remember the former things, those long ago; I am God, and there is no other; I am God, and there is none like me. I make known the end from the beginning, from ancient times, what is still to come. I say: My purpose will stand, and I will do all that I please." [92]

God not only declares the end from the

beginning but also integrates everything along the way. "works out everything in conformity with the purpose of his will," according to the apostle Paul.[93]

Meaning & Marveling

His redemptive plan brings significance to every practice, game, win, loss, rather than making us insignificant pawns in some cosmic chess game. Each of these sports experiences can advance God's plan and give God glory,

In this light, the apostle Paul states emphatically, "So whether you eat or drink or whatever you do, do it all for the glory of God."[94] Everything, even something as mundane as eating and drinking, is of concern to God in the way it does or doesn't bring him glory—this enjoyment and recognition of his greatness. As such, every bit of every one of our games, our practices, our winning and losing, is of great concern to God.

This is my answer. "Yes, he cares, but for very different reasons."

Do you see what this answer does? It exalts God as the One who alone can bring us what we want—this eternal glory—in the ways and at the time he wants us to experience it. We don't deny the desire. We are called to trust him to fulfill it.

This answer also brings clarity, unity, and meaning to things that concern us. Rather than seeing life as unimportant or important, sports as petty or not petty, we now see all of life on the important list, all aspects of life having the opportunity to show off God. Not just our sports, but certainly including our sports. "God doesn't waste anything. Every millisecond, every misery, in the path of obedience is producing an eternal weight of glory."[95]

This answer also leaves us marveling at such a great and gracious God. While life and sports are about him and his glory, he does include us as key players in fulfilling the purpose of enjoying and spreading that glory, in spite of our struggle to trust and yield to him. We are left marveling at one who would love us so much as to make every aspect of our lives a part of that good plan.

When this perspective has been grasped in the past, it has revolutionized people and cultures as it brings meaning to things the world called "petty" or unimportant. That revolution has produced some of the greatest literature, art, architecture, and music the world has ever seen as writers, artists, architects and builders, and composers and musicians did whatever they did all for the glory of God.

To all who are willing to ask this question, "Does God care who wins?" I ask you to lift up your eyes and behold this magnificent one who brings meaning to all of life, not only our games but our jobs, our finances, our relationships with others, and whatever else you want to add to the list...for his great glory and your great enjoyment. My hope in offering this answer and in making this appeal is that He would use it to spark a revolution in athletes, coaches and spectators that would produce the greatest sports the world has ever seen.

chapter five

Results

Results affect life trajectory.

Remember, I lost in a playoff at my first PGA Tour School. After that loss, I tried two more times to qualify for the Tour. I didn't get as close as that playoff loss either time.

The more distance I got from that day, the more I thought about how that loss significantly impacted my life. During the days, the weeks and months following that loss, I analyzed the events. I replayed the shots. The greater the analysis, the more I realized how close I came, and the reality of missing it hit home. This intensified my disappointment and my wrestling with feeling like a failure.

While results affect trajectory, the impact of that loss depended a great deal on my perspective. More than anything, I wanted to know if God cared about what happened.

If I said "no" and embraced the idea that

this golf game just didn't make it into the "God cares" bucket, I would be left alone in my disappointment about the outcome. Thinking this Tour School really didn't matter in the grand scheme of what God cares about, I would move myself and my golf away from God. That move would limit our relationship to the more "sacred" things of life, leaving my passion to win unchecked and untouched. It would also leave me alone to determine if I was a winner or a loser after this loss.

If I wanted to stay close to God, I would need to do something with this passion to win. Since he didn't care, then I shouldn't care. If and when I did care, I would need to purge this passion or hide it from God, since it was displeasing to him. I might even work to be "nicer" in my play rather than intense and passionate, but still be left on my own wondering how to view this playoff loss.

If I said a simple "yes" to the question and embraced the idea that God did care about this golf game, I would be left struggling with the reasons for my defeat. Why would God take me so close and then snatch away the victory? Did I do something wrong to bring this about? From the perspective that God rewards winners and punishes losers, I would have sought out the reasons for God's punishment and attempted to remove them so I could earn his favor for the next competition.

This leads to nothing but bondage and humiliation. I would be no different than I was in my life before I was a follower of Jesus. In my life up until then, my identity was tied to what I did, especially in sports. As a result, I always felt like a failure because, no matter how well I performed, it was never perfect. There were always faults to overcome, failures to deal with. Golf, more than any other sport I played, reminded me of that. In the inevitability and the futility of the process, I just kept trudging along trying to overcome those failures and establish what was lacking and fill the void. This wasn't true just in sports but in every arena of my life. I kept thinking one day I could get it right.

I knew the shame, the humiliation that comes from this perspective. I knew I "fell short," that something was wrong in me. This realization is part of what God used to draw me to himself and the good news of Christianity and invite me to follow him. I see now, that in my early years of our relationship, his unconditional love and my new identity in him had not worked its way fully into my soul as it related to my golf and performance. Back then, I tended to think that God cares and there must be things in me that caused him to not favor my performance. As a result, I left the loss that day trying harder and harder to impress God and win his approval while hiding more and more of what was going on in me, moving me—the real me—away from God.

You see, I knew that if God were looking for reasons to punish me, he didn't have to look far. I certainly had many, many character flaws and failures for him to choose from to disqualify me.

God's Relentless Pursuit

Instead, by God's grace and through this experience, he wouldn't let me keep this perspective. He wanted to resolve my glory struggle and deal with the humiliation I felt. He wanted to renew my mind and heal my heart.

He led me to several sources of understanding. I pressed into the Scriptures (some I have shared in this book) and into my soul for what I really believed and why. I prayed for wisdom. I talked with or read the writings of other followers of Christ, some whose thoughts I have shared here. Through these, God pushed me to think more deeply about the way I answer this question.

Along the way, I made this amazing discovery. I found that God has a passion for his and my glory that far exceeds my passion to win and the pursuit of my glory. I found that he is intensely desirous of tying me and others to this passion for his glory and he wants to connect every aspect of life, including winning and losing, to that glory.

As he showed me his passion, I saw that my passion is feeble. Mine is but a small sip and his passion is the great fountain from which we all drink. I discovered like C.S. Lewis, that "Our Lord finds our desires not too strong, but too weak. We are half-hearted creatures fooling around with drink and sex and ambition when infinite joy is offered to us, like an ignorant child who wants to go on making mud pies in a slum because he cannot image what is meant by the offer of a holiday at the sea. We are far too easily pleased."[96] This understanding of God changed my life, literally, and my golf in the process.

Instead of moving away from God because my passion was unimportant or something bad to squelch, I moved toward him as the source of my passion. There I found not rebuke but encouragement for my passion. I found that God wanted to stimulate my passion and reorient it toward the most satisfying of objects for that passion—his glory. I found that he wants to take half-hearted athletes like me who are fooling around with wins and our own glory and offer us the infinite joy of pursuing his glory through those same wins and losses. I found that he wants to tie everything, even in something as seemingly insignificant as hitting a little white ball around a grassy field to that glory. He has been at that stimulating and reorienting work in my heart (what I will call redeeming my heart) ever since, making more and more of his passion my passion and bringing meaning to more and more of my life.

Reorienting Our Trajectory

Another significant thing happened in the process. During those years, God was not only redeeming my heart, he was redeeming my sports. Golf became less and less a source of my identity while it became more and more a place for his glory to be pursued. I still worked hard and tried to win, but my motivation was different. I worked hard to express, not establish, the glory he restored in me as a golfer made in God's image. Losses still brought disappointment but didn't seem to have the devastating impact they previously had. I was able to embrace them more and more, as well as embrace the fewer "victories" (I mean a very loose definition of victory— certainly not tournament wins but making some money or even just playing well), as an expression of God's will for his glory in whichever came my way.

I don't want to imply this is easy. It isn't. Opening up my heart to this process has been one of the toughest challenges of my life.

But it has also been one of the most rewarding. As Beth and I wrestled with these concepts, our hearts were moved more and more toward others and God and less and less toward ourselves. During the four years of my pursuit of professional golf, Beth and I were also involved in helping others discover the life-giving truths of this Story of the Gospel. We also helped those who had embraced these truths grow deeper in their relationship with our Hero and his unique purpose for our lives.

While I struggled as a golfer, affirmation came in this role of helping people. Many encouraged us in different ways. Along the way, God seemed to be directing our efforts away from golf as a vocation and toward another vocation. We began to think about another purpose for our lives where this kind of involvement with others would be my primary vocation.[97] In the process, I left golf and returned to business not regretting one single aspect of our journey there.

Over the next three years, I wrestled with this question. "How do you, God, want us to uniquely pursue that glory in our vocation?" During that time, I studied, read, prayed, and talked to many others in trying to discern the answer. I became convinced that my next step was to work in a local church, helping people discover and grow in their relationship with Jesus Christ. I spent 8 years as an associate pastor, then 10 years as a church planter and pastor. Thirteen years ago, I began in my present role in sports ministry. We help local churches use the universal language of sports as a bridge to connect with people and as a laboratory to reveal hearts, both for the purpose of life transformation.

Transforming Sports

You might be wondering how my passion for winning and for the glory of God specifically looks these days. In my present day coaching and playing in various sports, I still want to win. I still try to win. I even pray for success. However, success for me isn't just about winning the game anymore. Success is no longer about establishing my glory, my greatness. Success is more about expressing God's glory in me. Success now is more about the expression and further unveiling of this restored glory that can happen in and through the competition—both in me and the others that I compete with. My prayers are oriented more for this kind of success. I find I pray in sports more and more, as Jesus taught, for his will to "be done on earth as it is in heaven."[98]

Applying this specifically, I pray for God to do what only he can do in and through this competition:

- To show me where my heart is still broken and how I am moving to establish my glory in competition
- To give me courage to be honest, really honest, and admit this wrong to him and any others that need to be informed

- To accept his forgiveness and love and to renew me to the truths surrounding his work to restore my glory
- To give me grace to move in this renewed attitude toward his glory
- To accept his will for the win or loss and look for how I might show off his character after either
- To give me a taste of the joy of glorifying him in my competition and in seeing others do the same through our competition
- To change my heart and heal my brokenness so that I long more and more for his glory not mine

These are just a few of the ways this reoriented passion continues to impact me. You may have others.

Integrating Glory

One thing is clear. However a stimulated and reoriented passion impacts someone, God wants it to spread. Over the years, what began with golf has moved to more and more areas of my life, where I attempt to live for his glory. The goal is whatever I do, to do it all for God's glory,[99] including but not exclusive to my sports as I play them now.

The breadth and depth of this idea astounds and overwhelms me at times. However, it is why he still cares about all of my wins and my losses even though they may seem much less significant now than they did then. He cares because he knows how every one of those wins and every one of those losses will affect the trajectory of my life, the lives of the other players, and the lives of those around me.

This goal—whatever I do to do it all for his glory—is the same goal that he has for every one of you reading this book. That is why he wanted this book written. Does God care about the writing? Absolutely, with greater passion than I ever will. However, he cares for very different reasons than I would apart from him. He cares about the question because the question is about him. He cares about how people answer the question because the answer moves people either away from or toward him. He cares about our answers because he wants us to reject the inadequate and unsatisfying ones and adopt the ones that and move us toward him as the one who alone can give us the wisdom we long for in asking the question. He cares about the answers because he wants to bring meaning to every aspect of our lives as they connect to his glory.

Honestly, that connection of doing whatever we do all for his glory is an unachievable goal in this Redemption Chapter of the Story. We may make progress, but the complete goal is out of reach for now. But not always. One day it will be achieved. In spite of that reality, God is not afraid to lay this goal before us because he knows the journey is worth it.

In that light, I am asking you to enter this journey. Maybe for the first time or maybe with a fresh and deeper sense of what you are entering,

- Think more seriously through your answer to the question and the reasons for your answer
- Pray to God—honestly and deeply about this question and your answers
- Acknowledge the frequency and depth of the self-centered pursuit of your own glory that is so often revealed in the laboratory of sports
- Turn from that self-centered pursuit to a more God-centered approach to sports that moves you and your sports toward God

- Connect your sports—playing, coaching, watching—to God and his glory
- Study the Redemption Story and our struggle for glory
- Pray for God to show you where you still struggle for your own glory in your sports
- Lay aside your "no" and adopt the "yes" answer with the different reasons that God has for winning and losing
- Pray for success in a different way, a higher way, than just winning the game
- Ask God to spread this perspective and passion to other areas of your life—work, family, marriage, etc.

You may recall I had three reasons for writing this book—to bring clarity to the confusion, to offer and stir respect in the interaction, and to move people toward God. My invitation to the journey involves all three.

My desire is not to end dialogue but to stimulate it. Many, many people have journeyed with me over the years. I am deeply grateful to them and for the way God has used them to help me in this process. As they have helped me, I have written hoping to be of some help to you. I hope you will also involve others in your journey.

Keep the dialogue going. If I haven't brought clarity, let me know. If I haven't shown respect, please point that out. If I can be of further help, I would count it a privilege to be included.

However you leave this book, my hope is that you will enter more fully this journey. Your decision about this invitation will impact your life going forward for results affect life trajectory.

God's glory and your joy are calling.

Acknowledgements

Teams can glorify God in a way that no individual can.

With this thought in mind, I have sought and received the amazing assistance of others throughout this project. Tim Briggs is responsible for planting the seed for writing this book. Our discussions over the years sharpened my thoughts and propelled me to put them on paper, originally as a series of blogs and now here. His investment in the book and his efforts to get the word out fueled my writing.

Carrie Givens is the editing force behind what you find here. Her experience and encouragement about the value of my written words really empowered me in times when I doubted what I was saying and the way I was saying it was of any worth.

These two are my teammates, my writing team, and I can't thank them enough for the different roles they played and all they have done to make this dream a reality. God knows it wouldn't have happened without you two.

There is also a long list of Kickstarter Backers—you know who you are—who invested in the idea of this book and in me. They were my cheerleaders, my supporters. Their overwhelmingly affirmative response brought this idea from a file on a computer to what you hold in your hands.

However, the team goes far beyond just those immediately involved. There have been people who have poured into me over the years to bring me to the place that I had the clarity of thought to offer this work. Wayne Dingler, Larry Whitehouse and John Stone personally mentored me and John Piper, Tim Keller, CS Lewis, Pat Conroy and John Eldredge did so through their writings. Their fingerprints are found on almost every page.

Others have been colleagues and friends who have affirmed my calling and gifts— Ken Helton, Jim Elliff, Dennis Hickey, Wes Priestley, Brian Long, Bob Dyar, Palmer Trice, Frank Reich, Steve Heffner, Tim Sittema, Sam Blumenthal, Ken Samuelson, Jay Carter, Clay

Claiborne, Rusty Reed, Whit Wilks, Tommy Worth, Jake Puryear, Dave Huber, ML Woodruff, Scott Tyson, Evan Albertyn, Greg Linville, Tim Conrad, Jeff Fox, Ken Cross, the Lost & Found class, and Jay Martin. This list also includes my children—Katie, John, Scott, and Brian. Every time I offer those gifts, including here, I see you standing behind me, urging me on.

There are two others I must also mention. The first is my wife, Beth. She introduced me to this great and glorious God as revealed in the gospel of His Son. I had never met anyone who said they were a Christian before Beth did. I snagged her and our marriage of over 40 years has been the most significant environment where I have learned more about Him and his beauty. I am what I am today because of that introduction and that environment. Beth, you are my best friend and supporter, my best reviewer, my most stimulating interacter whose English advice I take without exception. Thank you for that introduction, your part in the environment, and your love and support over the years. Your input is on every page, and I wouldn't be who I am without you.

Last, I must mention the One this book

is really about. There is no book without him. There is no author to write that book. There is no Story from which these thoughts echo. The Community of the Godhead is the team that this team seeks to glorify in our writing.

You may have noticed one theme in these acknowledgements. Courage. I easily waver. I needed a lot of it to get to this point. The affirmation and passion of the Lord Jesus Christ for me and for his glory are ultimately what gave me the courage to write. It was his voice behind all these other voices I mention. Without him, I am lost.

About the Author

Bob Schindler is the Director of Cede Partners, an initiative of Cede Sports, where he has served since 2003. Prior to that, Bob was an Associate Pastor for eight years and a church planter and Senior Pastor for 10 years in East Tennessee. In both churches, Bob started sports ministries that served both adults and children and were the primary outreach vehicle for both churches. Before entering the ministry as a vocation, Bob played professional golf for four years and was in business for six years, in both the chemical and software industries. Bob studied Chemical Engineering at Vanderbilt University and is currently pursuing his Masters in Religion with an emphasis in Christian Thought at Gordon-Conwell Theological Seminary in Charlotte, NC. Bob is married to Beth, his wife of 40 years, and has six grown children (one daughter, three sons, two daughters-in-law) and three grandchildren. They have called Church at Charlotte home since 2003 and have been supported missionaries of the church since 2008.

Notes

Introduction

[1] John Feinstein, *Tales from Q School: Inside Golf's Fifth Major* (New York: Little, Brown, 2007). 7-8.

Chapter One

[2] Michael Morris, "Clemson Coach Dabo Swinney on CFP Win: 'Only God Can Do This'," *CNS News Blog*, January 10, 2017, http://www.cnsnews.com/blog/michael-morris/coach-dabo-swinney-clemsons-win-only-god-can-do.

[3] Kara Yorio, "Does God Care Who Wins the Super Bowl?" *The Daily Gazette News*, January 27, 2014, https://dailygazette.com/article/2014/01/22/does-god-care-who-wins-super-bowl.

[4] Mike Fiammetta, "Aaron Rodgers: 'I don't think God cares' about game outcomes," *SI.com*, January 20, 2015, https://www.si.com/nfl/2015/01/20/aaron-rodgers-i-dont-think-god-cares-outcomes-football-games.

5   Ibid.

6   Lee Warren, "Does God care who wins?," *The Pathway*, February 22, 2005, http://mbcpathway.com/2005/03/29/article19744-htm/.

7   Ibid.

8   Mark Oppenheimer, "In the Fields of the Lord," *SI.com*, February 4, 2013, https://www.si.com/vault/2013/02/04/106280215/in-the-fields-of-the-lord.

9   Kara Yorio, "Does God Care Who Wins the Super Bowl?"

10   There appears to be a trend in recent years toward the "no" answer. 2015 Research by Lifeway seems to indicate that to be a strong trend with 90% of Americans giving the "no" answer to the question. This research is found at http://blog.lifeway.com/newsroom/2016/02/03/does-god-decide-care-who-wins-the-super-bowl/.

11   Talo Steves, "Putting Faith and Sports into Perspective," *Total Blue Sports*, November 27, 2007, http://www.scout.com/college/byu/story/706030-putting-faith-and-sports-into-perspective.

12   John Walters, "Does God care who wins the Super Bowl?," *KSL.com*, January 30, 2009, https://www.ksl.com/?sid=5465537.

13   Dick Harmon, "Collie calls reaction to his post-game comments 'ridiculous'," *Deseret News,* November 27, 2007, http://www.deseretnews.com/

article/695231106/Collie-calls-reaction-to-his-post-game-comments-ridiculous.html.

14 John Blake, "When did God become a sports fan?," *CNN.com*, last modified May 25, 2010, http://www.cnn.com/2010/LIVING/wayoflife/05/25/God.sports/.

15 1 Cor. 13:12

16 Ps. 96:3

Chapter Two

17 Dana Scarton, "Christianity in Sports," *Salina Journal*, October 4, 1991, https://www.newspapers.com/newspage/26324767/.

18 Michael Brown, "Does God Care Who Wins the Super Bowl?" *The Christian Post*, February 3, 2015, http://www.christianpost.com/news/does-god-care-who-wins-the-super-bowl-133497/print.html.

19 John Walters, "Does God care who wins the Super Bowl?"

20 "What Does Jesus Have to Do with Sports?" *The Locker Room* (blog), March 2, 2015, https://active-faithsports.com/blogs/the-locker-room/17560132-what-does-jesus-have-to-do-with-sports.

21 John Walters, "Does God care who wins the Super Bowl?"

22 Ibid.

23 Mark Oppenheimer, "In the Fields of the Lord."

24 Ibid.

25 *Coach John Wooden Quotes* (blog), February 17, 2011, http://coachjohnwoodenquotes.blogspot.com/2011/02/sports-do-not-build-character-they.html.

26 John Walters, "Does God care who wins the Super Bowl?"

27 Daniel Schorn, "Transcript: Tom Brady, Part 3," *60 Minutes*, November 4, 2005, http://www.cbsnews.com/news/transcript-tom-brady-part-3/.

28 Matt. 10:30

29 Lam. 3:22-23

30 Col. 1:16-17

31 Col. 1:18

32 C.S. Lewis. "Christianity and Culture," in *Christian Reflections*, ed. Walter Hooper. (Grand Rapids: Wm. B. Eerdman's Publishing Co., 2014), 41.

33 John 7:37-38

Chapter Three

34 Rob Demovsky, "Aaron Rodgers: I Think God Was a Packers Fan Tonight," September 21, 2015, http://abc13.com/sports/aaron-rodgers-i-think-god-was-a-packers-fan-tonight/994160/.

35 Jason McIntyre, "Russell Wilson: God Set Up the NFC Championship, Making it "so dramatic, so rewarding, so special," *The Big Lead*, January 20, 2015, http://thebiglead.com/2015/01/20/russell-wilson-god-set-up-the-nfc-championship-making-

it-so-dramatic-so-rewarding-so-special/.

[36] Cobus Kruger, "Drop goal legend Jannie de Beer's example of obedient faith," *Gateway News*, November 11, 2015, http://gatewaynews.co.za/drop-goal-legend-jannie-de-beers-example-of-obedient-faith-in-action/.

[37] Wilson tweeted after the Seahawks loss to the New England Patriots in Super Bowl IVIX – "Thank You God for the opportunity. We'll be back... I will never waiver [sic] on who He has called me to be..." according to http://insider.foxnews.com/2015/02/02/russell-wilson-thanks-god-promises-keep-evolving-after-super-bowl-loss.

[38] Ed Uszynsk, "Does God Care Who Wins?," Desiring God, January 30, 2015, http://www.desiringgod.org/articles/does-god-care-about-who-wins.

[39] John Walters, "Does God care who wins the Super Bowl?"

[40] Ed Uszynsk, "Does God Care Who Wins?"

[41] Matt. 5:3

[42] 2 Cor. 8:9

[43] Heb. 11:33-34

[44] Heb. 11:35-37

[45] Heb. 11:39

[46] Heb. 11:34

[47] Timothy Keller, *The Meaning of Marriage* (New York: Riverhead Books, 2011), 44.

[48] Philip Yancey, *What's So Amazing About Grace?* (New

York: Harper Collins, 1997), 67.

[49] Is. 55:9

[50] Ed Uszynsk, "Does God Care Who Wins?"

[51] Timothy Keller, *The Meaning of Marriage*, 44.

[52] James 4:13-15

[53] 1 Peter 5:5

[54] Rebecca Reynolds. Facebook post, accessed January 10, 2017. https://www.facebook.com/permalink.php?story_fbid=397882627226368&id=100010139014640

[55] Rebecca Reynolds, Ibid.

[56] Timothy Keller, *The Meaning of Marriage*, 44.

Chapter Four

[57] For more on glory, see *The Weight of Glory* by C.S. Lewis (available from HarperOne, an imprint of HarperCollins Publishers, as *The Weight of Glory and Other Addresses*, 2009). He goes much more into these two facets of glory.

[58] Vince Lombardi, https://www.goodreads.com/quotes/108267-if-winning-isn-t-everything-why-do-they-keep-score

[59] Mia Hamm, https://www.brainyquote.com/quotes/quotes/m/miahamm204540.html

[60] Tiger Woods, https://www.brainyquote.com/quotes/quotes/t/tigerwoods368920.html

[61] Charles Barkley, https://www.brainyquote.com/quotes/quotes/c/charlesbar454164.html

62 The Westminster Shorter Catechism, The Westminster Presbyterian, accessed May 9, 2017, http://www.westminsterconfession.org/confessional-standards/the-westminster-shorter-catechism.php.

63 This is the first line of *The Purpose Driven Life*, by Rick Warren (Philadelphia: Running Press, 2003).

64 Frederick Buechner, *Telling the Truth: The Gospel as Tragedy, Comedy, and Fairy Tale* (New York: HarperCollins, 1977) 91.

65 Randy Pope, *The Answer: Putting an End to the Search for Life Satisfaction* (Duluth, GA: Life on Life Resources, 2005).

66 Matt Chandler refers to these four chapters as "The Gospel from the Air" in *The Explicit Gospel* (Wheaton, IL: Crossway, 2012). In *The Story*, a film presented by SpreadTruth, the four chapters are referred to as Creation, The Fall, The Rescue, The Restoration (http://www.thestoryfilm.com). Ed Stetzer refers to this as "The Big Story of Scripture" (http://www.christianitytoday.com/edstetzer/2012/november/big-story-of-scripture-creation-fall-redemption.html) and references Trevin Wax's *Counterfeit Gospels: Rediscovering the Good News in a World of False Hope*, which calls the chapters Creation, Fall, Redemption, and Restoration (Chicago: Moody Publishers, 2011).

67 Gen. 1:1

68 Cornelius Plantinga Jr. *Engaging God's World: A*

Christian Vision of Faith, Learning, and Living (Grand Rapids: Wm. B. Eerdmans Publishing Co., 2002), 22.

[69] Gen. 1:26-27

[70] Ps. 8:5, Heb. 2:7

[71] While being made in the image of God has many facets, this giving of ourselves to others is one of them. "Because God is the Continuous Outpourer, we bear his image as continuous outpourers. Being made in the image of God means that we were created to act the way God acts, having been given a nature with which such behavior is natural." – Harold Best in *Unceasing Worship* (Downer's Grove, IL: InterVarsity Press, 2003), 23.

[72] Rom.. 3:23

[73] Randy Pope, *The Answer.*

[74] C.S. Lewis, *The Weight of Glory and Other Addresses*, 37.

[75] Gen. 3:16-19

[76] C.S. Lewis, *Mere Christianity in The Complete C.S. Lewis Signature Classics* (Grand Rapids: Zondervan, 2007), 49.

[77] Philip Yancey, *The Jesus I Never Knew* (New York: HarperCollins, 1995), 268.

[78] Gen. 12:1-3

[79] Mark 10:45

[80] Phil. 2:6-8

[81] Luke 19:10

82   Heb. 2:10

83   Philip Yancey, *The Jesus I Never Knew*, 268.

84   Rev. 21:5

85   Col. 1:27

86   Rev. 21:4

87   For example, Randy Alcorn and John Piper both think there will be sports/games in the New Heavens and Earth, what we may think of as Heaven.

88   Rom. 8:18

89   John Piper, *Brothers We are Not Professionals* (Nashville: B&H Publishing Group, 2002), 5-6.

90   Ed Uszynsk, "Does God Care Who Wins?"

91   Rev. 21:5

92   Is. 46:9-10

93   Eph. 1:11

94   1 Cor. 10:31

95   Interview with John Piper, *Desiring God*, December 2, 2015, http://www.desiringgod.org/interviews/your-suffering-is-working-for-you.

Chapter Five

96   C.S. Lewis, *The Weight of Glory and Other Addresses*, 26.

97   Some would call this occupation the "ministry." I like to refer to it as vocational ministry, since I believe all followers of Jesus are ministers.

98   Matt. 6:10

99   1 Cor. 10:31

CPSIA information can be obtained
at www.ICGtesting.com
Printed in the USA
JSHW050704251122
33695JS00004B/13

9 780999 126509